Fun to do

BEADS, BADGES & BANGLES

Clare Beaton

CONTENTS

Swallow

What You Will Need

Before you begin to make jewellery it is a good idea to get ready a few useful tools. You will need a pencil, eraser and ruler for drawing and marking out, and a compass is handy for measuring perfect circles. For cutting paper, thin card or fabric, you can use a pair of round-ended scissors or pinking shears, but you will need to ask a grown up to cut thick card for you with a craft knife. You can use glue or tape to fix things together, and you will need a needle and thread ready for sewing. Paint and felt-tip pens are needed for decorating. Some of the finished projects will need a light coat of varnish.

modelling tool

PVA glue and spreader

paint

felt-tip pens

paint-brushes

needles

double-sided tape

masking tape

rolling-pin

pins

clear tape

Other Useful Things

All sorts of things come in useful for making jewellery. Start a collection and keep adding to it. Store useful odds and ends in a box. Your collection might include:

Plastic bottles, textured plastic packaging, cardboard tubes, yoghurt cartons, bottle tops, jar lids, old newspapers, corrugated cardboard, coloured card and coloured paper, gold and silver card, gummed paper, crêpe paper, tissue-paper, wool, string, gold and silver thread, elastic, cellophane and foil sweet wrappers, broken bead necklaces, tinsel, glitter, self-adhesive stickers, buttons, sequins, felt, material off-cuts, hair slides, hairbands, safety pins.

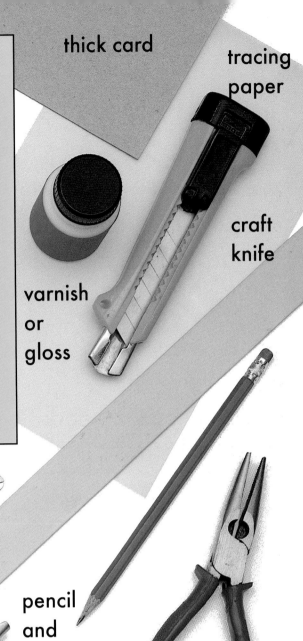

thick card

tracing paper

craft knife

varnish or gloss

compass

scissors

metal ruler

pencil and eraser

thread

pliers

pinking shears

Remember

☆ Wear an apron and cover the work area.
☆ Collect together the items in the materials box at the beginning of each project.
☆ Always ask an adult for help when you see this sign [!]
☆ Clear up after yourself.

ruler

What a Corker!

Save up used corks to make this beautiful necklace. Alternatively corks can be cheaply bought from shops that sell wine-making equipment.

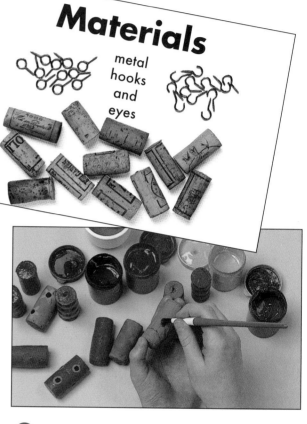

Materials

metal hooks and eyes

12 corks

1 Hold the corks at each end and paint using about 3 different base colours. Stand the painted corks on one end, paint the other end and leave to dry. Turn over and paint the other end the same colour.

2 Decorate the painted corks with patterns in contrasting colours making them as bright as you can. Leave to dry.

3 Lightly varnish the painted corks and leave to dry.

4 Screw a hook and an eye into either end of 9 of the corks.

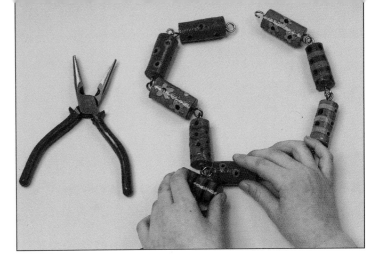

5 Join these 9 corks together. Use pliers to close up the hooks, but leave the last hook open so that the necklace can be put on easily.

6 Make a pendant by joining together the remaining 3 corks. Hook the pendant onto the necklace.

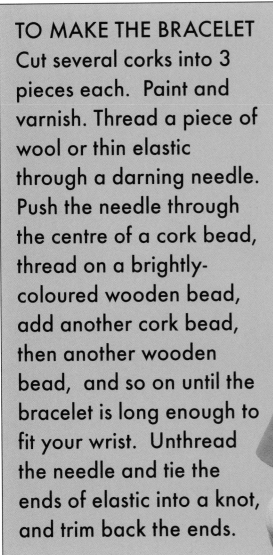

TO MAKE THE BRACELET
Cut several corks into 3 pieces each. Paint and varnish. Thread a piece of wool or thin elastic through a darning needle. Push the needle through the centre of a cork bead, thread on a brightly-coloured wooden bead, add another cork bead, then another wooden bead, and so on until the bracelet is long enough to fit your wrist. Unthread the needle and tie the ends of elastic into a knot, and trim back the ends.

Robot Badges

An opportunity to use lots of bits and pieces – collect anything silver and gold and create your own robotic characters.

Materials

matchbox, gold plastic bottle cap, safety pin, 2 gold stars, 2 paper fasteners, sequins, 1 metal buttton, silver card, silver foil, gold paper

1 Cover a matchbox with silver foil leaving one end unwrapped. Pull down the cardboard flap at the open end and cut off. Push the matchbox back in.

2 Cut a semi-circle of gold paper. Cut a fringe along the curved edge.

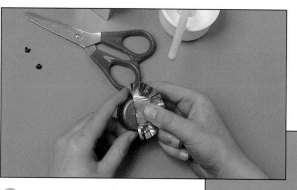

3 Glue the fringed semi-circle onto the back of the bottle cap. Stick 2 sequins inside the bottle cap to make the robot's eyes.

4 Push the bottle cap head firmly into the open end of the matchbox.

6

! **5** Use a scissor blade to make a small slit a third of the way down each side of the matchbox. Push a long paper fastener into each hole to make the robot's arms.

6 To make the robot's legs cut 2 pieces of thin silver card 1 cm x 3 cm and fold over 1 cm to make the feet. Glue to the back of the matchbox.

7 Decorate the front of the robot with the stars, sequins and button.

8 Tape a safety pin to the back of the robot and it is ready to wear.

Make a robot from a large matchbox which can be opened to keep small teasures in.

7

Bottle Bracelets

Recycle plastic bags and bottles to make these stunning bracelets. Wash out the bottles thoroughly first, and soak off the labels in warm, soapy water.

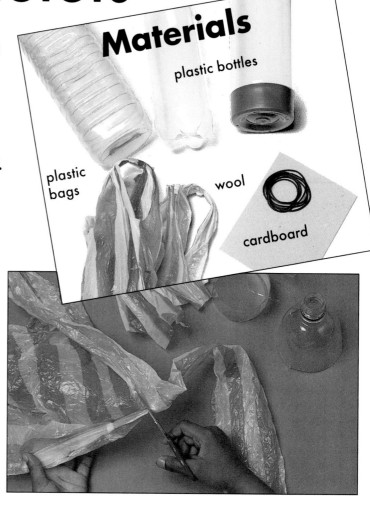

Materials

plastic bottles

plastic bags

wool

cardboard

! **1** Cut a 4-cm wide band from a round plastic bottle. Trim the edges with scissors. Try it on over your hand – if it is too big, cut and re-join with tape to fit.

2 Cut a plastic bag into strips roughly 5 cm wide.

3 Wind the strips around the plastic band securing each piece with a small piece of tape, until the bracelet looks well-padded.

4 To make the pom pom, cut 2 discs from cardboard measuring 5 cm in diameter with a 1.5 cm hole in the centre.

8

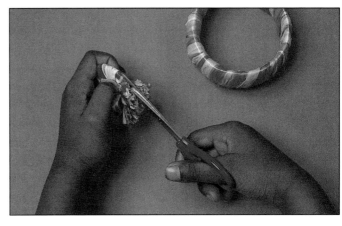

5 Cut striped plastic bags into thin strips. Wrap these around the card 'doughnut' until there are several layers of plastic covering it.

6 Use a pair of scissors to cut through the plastic along the edge of the cardboard rings.

7 Tie a long piece of wool securely around the plastic between the 2 cardboard rings and knot tightly. Cut through the cardboard rings and remove. Fluff up the pom pom and tie it onto the bottle bracelet. Trim off the ends of the wool.

Autumn Leaf Necklace

A *super seasonal necklace made from bits of card and a few beads.*

Materials

9 wooden beads

corrugated cardboard

wool

1 Trace off the leaf templates on page 31 and draw 3 of each onto the corrugated card. Cut out.

2 Paint the leaves on both sides, using about 3 different base colours. Leave to dry.

3 Paint vein patterns onto the leaves in contrasting colours and leave to dry.

4 Lightly varnish the leaves on one side. Leave to dry, then turn over and varnish the other side.

5 Thread some wool onto a darning needle, making sure that it is long enough to go over your head. Push the needle through the back of the leaf close to the top edge. Thread on a bead, then push the needle back out through the front of the leaf.

6 Continue to thread on the leaves and the beads. When they are all threaded on, make sure there is an equal amount of wool left at each end and knot the ends together.

You could also make a summer shell necklace using the templates on page 31, threaded together with pearls rather than beads.

11

Materials

12 large pasta tubes

red and yellow card

feathers

8 beads

self-adhesive dots

large plastic pot with rim

string

Apache Fun

A tooth necklace and feather armband that are perfect for dressing up.

Tooth necklace

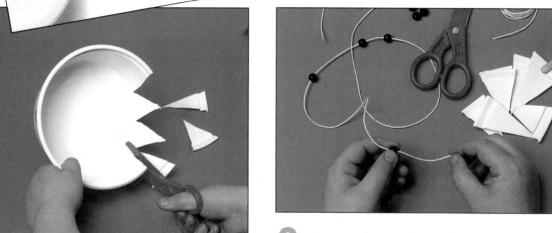

1 Cut 7 triangular 'teeth' from a large plastic pot cutting down from the rim.

2 Thread the beads onto a long piece of string. Run some glue under the rim of a tooth and stick onto the string between the middle 2 beads.

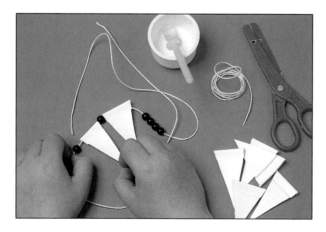

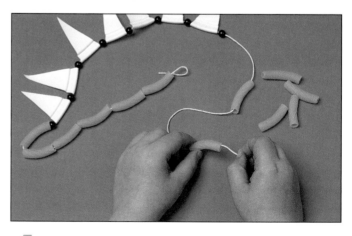

3 Continue to stick the teeth between the beads until they have all been used.

4 Thread 6 large pasta tubes onto either side of the string and knot the ends of the string together.

Feather armband

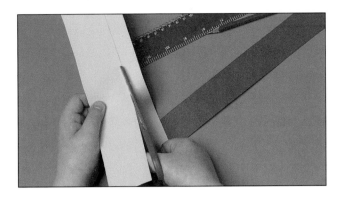

5 Cut a piece of red card 4 cm wide and long enough to go around your upper arm including a 4 cm overlap. Cut a strip of yellow card the same length and 2 cm wide.

6 Use pinking shears to cut out a zig zag along one edge of the yellow card and glue onto the red card. Stick black dots on each of the yellow triangles.

7 Cut off a long piece of black and/or white string and glue onto the red card, following the zig zag pattern of the yellow card. Turn the card over and tape feathers along the bottom (string) edge.

You could make a feather headband too. Use double-sided tape to fix the headband and armband in place.

Snake Charmers

Sssssensational snakes to slither up your arms or hook over your ears.

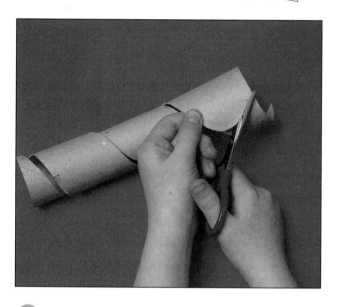

Materials

self-adhesive dots

2 sequins

gummed paper

large cardboard tube

Snake armband

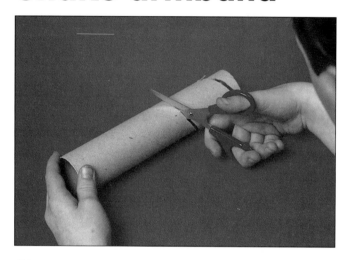

1 Cut the cardboard tube into a spiral about 5 cm wide. Straighten out gently and neaten the edges with scissors.

2 Cut one end rounded for the head. Leave the other end pointed for the tail.

3 Paint the outside of the spiral green and leave to dry.

4 Tear the gummed paper into strips and use to decorate the spiral. Fold the ends of the paper over the edges of the card.

14

5 Stick small dots all over the snake's body to decorate. Stick 2 large dots onto the head for eyes and glue sequins into the centre of them.

Ear snake

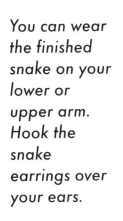

6 Trace off 2 snakes onto white card using the template on page 31. Cut out and paint.

7 Decorate with self-adhesive dots.

You can wear the finished snake on your lower or upper arm. Hook the snake earrings over your ears.

15

Robin Hood Pouch

A simple-to-make money bag that can be hung from your belt or around your neck.

Materials

green felt

1 metre of cord

large wooden bead

painted cardboard leaf (from page 10)

1 Use a compass to draw a 24-cm diameter circle onto a piece of paper. Draw another circle within it of 20 cm diameter.

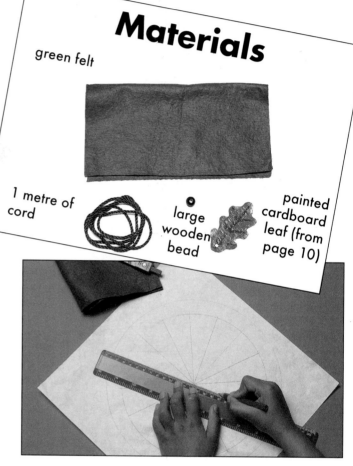

2 Divide the inner circle up into 16 equal sections.

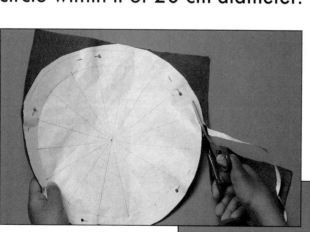

3 Roughly trim down the paper around the circle and pin onto the felt. Cut around the outer circle.

4 Before unpinning the paper, poke a pin through each of the 16 points marked on the inner circle and mark with a pen dot on the felt. Unpin the paper.

5 Fold in half along each of the marked dots in turn and cut tiny slits, just large enough to thread the cord through to make a drawstring.

6 Begin to thread the cord through the holes. Thread on the painted leaf (*instructions for making on page 10*) between the 8th and the 9th hole.

7 When you have threaded the cord through all the holes, pull the ends together and ease the felt into a pouch shape.

8 Thread the cord ends through a snugly-fitting bead and knot the ends together. To close the pouch push the bead down.

You can make a pretty, party purse and decorate it with sequins and beads.

Badges For Everyone!

These bright badges are made from layers of newspaper pasted onto a shaped card.

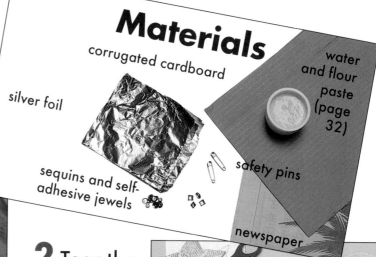

Materials

corrugated cardboard

silver foil

sequins and self-adhesive jewels

safety pins

water and flour paste (page 32)

newspaper

1 Trace off the heart and star templates on page 31 onto corrugated card, and cut out.

The sheriff star

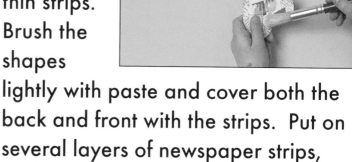

2 Tear the newspaper into short, thin strips. Brush the shapes lightly with paste and cover both the back and front with the strips. Put on several layers of newspaper strips, pasting in between. Leave to dry.

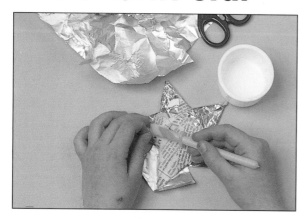

3 Cover the star in silver foil, pressing carefully around the edges and gluing in place at the back.

4 Roll 5 balls of foil and attach to the star points with tape.

18

The heart

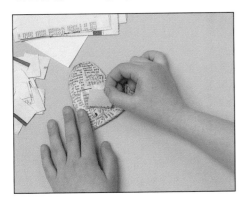

5 Add more layers of newspaper to the centre of the heart to give a ballooning effect. Leave to dry.

6 Paint the base colour. When this is dry, paint on patterns in contrasting colours. Once dry cover with a light coat of varnish.

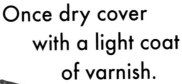

7 Once the varnish has dried, stick on jewels and sequins to decorate.

Tape safety pins to the back of the finished badges and they are ready to wear. You can also use the smaller templates on page 31 to make beautiful brooches. Decorate in the same way as the badges and tape gold thread between the decorated shapes.

Out of This World

Re-use old plastic bottles and packaging for effects that are out of this world.

The badge

1 Cut a circle from the metallic paper to fit snugly into the plastic lid. Secure with a dab of glue.

Materials

safety pin

paper fastener

metallic paper

moulded plastic

self-adhesive stars

white paper

plastic lid with lip

silver spray paint

2 large plastic bottles

2 Cut a star out of white paper and stick in the centre of the metallic paper.

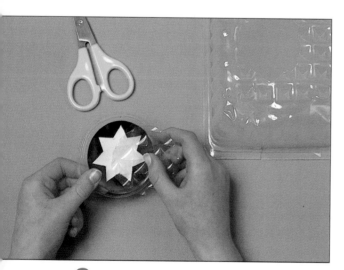

3 Cut a circle from the moulded plastic to fit snugly into the plastic lid and place on top of the star.

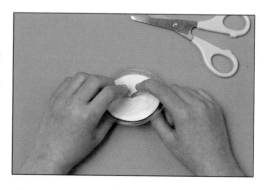

[!] 4 Pierce a hole in the centre of your junk sandwich with the end of a scissor blade. Push the paper fastener through the hole and open out at the back.

The gauntlets

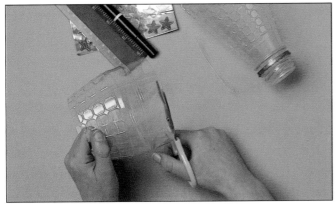

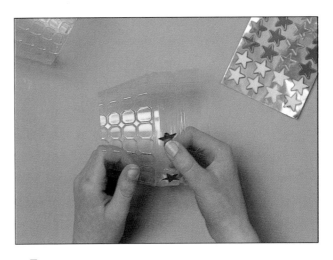

!**5** Mark 2 lines 7.5 cm and 15 cm from the neck of the bottles. Cut along these lines and trim the rough edges with scissors.

6 Stick two rows of stars around the wider end of the bottles.

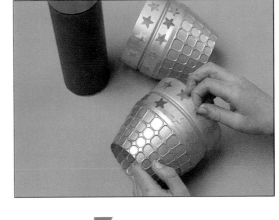

Tape a safety pin to the back of the badge and pin it onto your top. Slip the gauntlets over your hands and prepare for blast off.

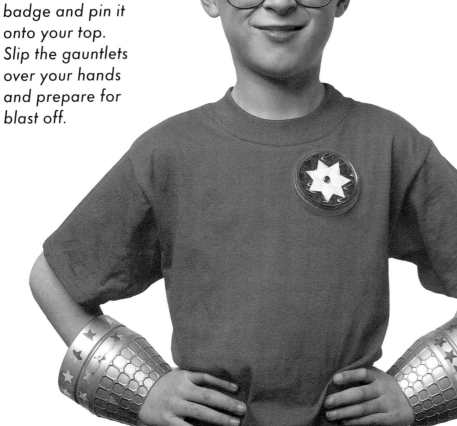

7 Spray all over with silver spray paint. When the paint has dried completely carefully remove the stars.

Sparkly Garland

Don't just decorate the tree this Christmas. Why not decorate yourself too?

1 Cut 5 10-cm lengths from the silver tinsel and 5 10-cm lengths from the red tinsel. Cut 10 2-cm lengths of double-sided tape.

2 Fold each piece of tinsel in half and press a piece of double-sided tape onto it.

3 Attach a piece of silver tinsel 25 cm in from the end of the gold string by removing the backing from the double-sided tape and folding the tinsel around the string. Position all the silver tinsel pieces along the string about 10 cm apart from each other.

4 Cut 8 30-cm lengths from the gold ribbon. Tie 2 pieces onto the gold string between each piece of silver tinsel.

5 Push the gold ribbon close to the tinsel. Curl the ribbon with closed scissor blades.

Stick coloured tinsel onto hair slides, combs and hairbands to make some stunning sparkly bits for your hair.

6 Finally add the red tinsel pieces. Remove the backing of the double-sided tape and fold onto the gold string between the gold ribbons.

7 Knot the ends of the string together.

Animal Badges

These animal badges are made from salt dough, which can be modelled into any shape you choose.

Materials

100 g plain flour

50 g salt

80 ml water

safety pins

1 teaspoon cooking oil

1 Mix together the salt, flour and cooking oil in a bowl. Add the water a little at a time and mix to a smooth paste.

2 Turn the dough out onto a lightly-floured board. Knead and roll out to about ½ cm thick. Cut out some animal shapes.

3 Add salt dough eyes, wings or fins. Model the dough, brush lightly with a little water and press down firmly onto the animal shapes.

!4 Add decorative details. Place the finished badges onto a lightly-greased baking tray and bake in the oven on the lowest setting overnight.

5 Paint the animal shapes in bright colours and leave to dry.

6 Add detail with a fine paint-brush, or felt-tip pens. Once dry, seal all over with a light coat of varnish.

Tape a safety pin to the back of the badges and they are ready to wear.

ANIMAL WALLHANGING
Make some other animal shapes – why not try zoo animals this time. Decorate and varnish them and glue them to a long piece of felt. Hang it up in your room.

Flowers For Your Hair

Materials

crêpe paper (dark pink, pink, yellow, green)

green wire

safety pin

A corsage that will stay as fresh as the day you make it.

1 Mark out circles measuring about 10 cm in diameter onto the crêpe paper. You will need 6 yellow and a total of 9 light and dark pink circles. Cut out. You can use pinking shears for decorative effect.

2 Place 3 circles of crêpe paper on top of each other. Fold in half. Hold in the centre and pinch together between thumb and forefinger.

3 Wind about 10 cm of wire around the base of the flower head. Twist the ends together and press close to the flower.

4 Cut a 5-cm wide strip of green crêpe paper. Cut a zig zag pattern along one edge to make the leaves. Cut into sections of 4 leaves long.

26

5 Wind a leaf section around the base of the flower head and secure with the end of a 15-cm length of wire. Leave the rest of the wire hanging down.

6 Cover the top of the wire with a piece of green crêpe paper 4 cm x 2 cm backed with double-sided tape: remove the backing and wind around pressing firmly together.

7 Once you have made all 5 flowers, hold together in a bunch. Wind the stem of one flower around the rest to keep in place.

Attach the bunch of flowers to a hat or a piece of clothing with a safety pin fastened inside the item of clothing. Individual flowers can be wound around a hairband or hair comb for a very pretty effect.

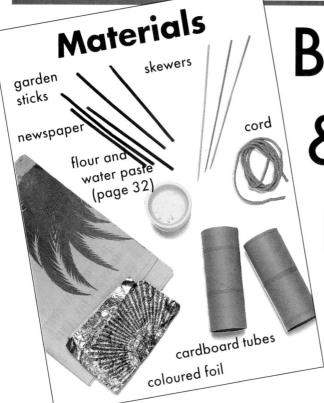

Materials

garden sticks

skewers

newspaper

flour and water paste (page 32)

cord

cardboard tubes

coloured foil

Beads, Beads & More Beads

Lots of different beads to make. Thread them onto string, wool, elastic, or even an old shoelace.

Papier mâché pulp beads

1 Tear newspaper into stamp-size squares and put into a bowl. Cover with warm water and leave to soak for 24 hours.

2 Squeeze the water from the paper and drain. Add a little paste and mix well to form a mush.

3 Take small balls of mush and form into large beads around the garden sticks.

! **4** Slide the balls carefully off the sticks and place onto an old baking tray. Leave in the oven overnight on its lowest setting to dry out thoroughly.

5 Thread the beads back onto the sticks. Pierce the end of the sticks into a lump of play dough, making sure that the beads are not touching each other. Decorate with paint, then varnish. Slide the beads off the sticks once dry.

Paper beads

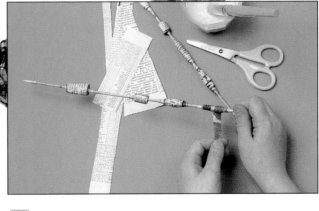

6 Cut newspaper into strips of different widths and lengths, including some pennant-shaped strips. The longer the strip the larger the bead will be.

7 Put paste on one side of the paper strips and wind glue-side down around the skewers. Gently pull the beads off the skewers and leave to dry.

Continues on next page

8 Thread the beads back onto the skewers and stick into a ball of play dough. Paint the beads all over and leave to dry. Use several different base colours.

9 Decorate the beads by painting on patterns in contrasting colours and by sticking on strips of coloured foil. When dry, slide the beads off the skewers.

Cardboard beads

10 Paint and decorate the tubes. When dry cover with a light coat of varnish and leave to dry.

11 Cut open the tubes and paint the insides black. When dry, cut into 2-cm wide sections.

12 Tape the painted sections into circles once again, linking them as you go to make a chain.

Templates

Here are all the templates you will need to make the projects in this book. Simply trace around the required outline using tracing paper or greaseproof paper, and transfer onto paper or card. Alternatively, you could make a template from thick card that can be used time and time again. For instructions on how to do this turn to page 32.

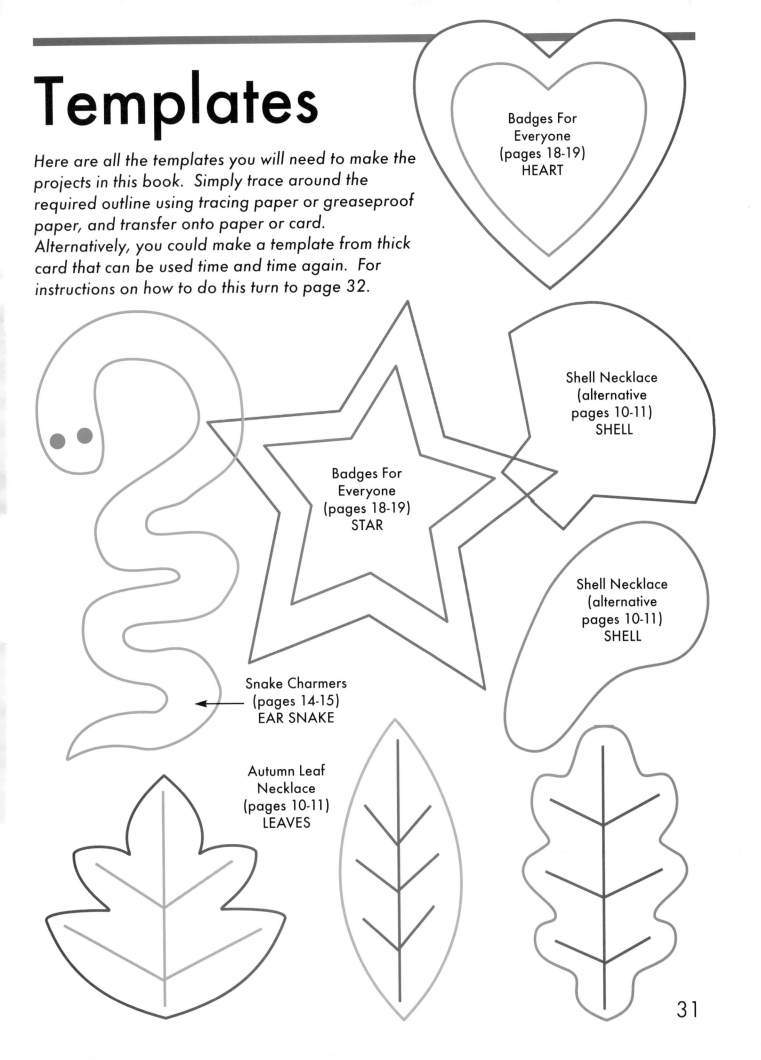

Badges For
Everyone
(pages 18-19)
HEART

Shell Necklace
(alternative
pages 10-11)
SHELL

Badges For
Everyone
(pages 18-19)
STAR

Shell Necklace
(alternative
pages 10-11)
SHELL

Snake Charmers
(pages 14-15)
EAR SNAKE

Autumn Leaf
Necklace
(pages 10-11)
LEAVES

Advice to Parents

This book is full of exciting ideas for turning junk into beautiful items of jewellery. Some of the projects are quick to make, others need some advance preparation, so do plan in advance. Work on several projects at a time, so that your child does not lose interest waiting for paint to dry, dough to bake, or varnish to set.

Tools and Materials

Paint From a small selection of paints – red, yellow, blue, black and white – all other colours can be obtained by mixing. Encourage your child to explore colour mixing for herself. Poster paints are ideal for painting all the projects in this book. Always ensure that paint has dried before going on to the next step in the project.

Felt-tip pens A set of felt-tip pens is a good idea for adding fine decorative details to jewellery.

Glue Solvent-free PVA adhesive is recommended as it is versatile, clean, strong and safe.

Double-sided tape This tape is very strong. It is rather expensive but worth every penny. If you use it carefully it will go a long way. It comes in rolls in various widths and can be bought at a stationer's or art and craft shop.

Scissors For the sake of safety children should use small scissors with round-ended metal blades and plastic handles. Although these are fine for cutting paper and thin card, they will not cut thick card and this is best done by you. This will often require a craft knife. Use a metal ruler to provide a straight cutting edge. If you do not have a cutting mat, use an old chopping board or very thick card to protect the work surface beneath. Regularly change the craft knife blade for a clean, sharp cut. Pinking shears are fun to use as they give an interesting zig zag edge to paper and fabric.

Varnish A light coat of varnish will give finished items of jewellery a shiny finish and a protective coat that will help them to last longer. You should buy non-toxic varnish that is suitable for children to use, available from most art and craft shops. Alternatively watered-down PVA glue can be used. Always ensure that the varnish has completely dried before adding any decorations.

Jewellery fitments If you wish, it is possible to buy jewellery fitments such as brooch pins, earring clips and necklace safety catches from art and craft shops.

Salt Dough

To make this versatile modelling medium you can use either brown or white plain flour. In the recipe given on page 18 only a rough guide to the amount of water needed is provided. It is important to add the water a little at a time, until the salt dough leaves the bowl and hands clean. If the dough becomes slightly tacky, add a little flour and work it into the mixture. Use salt dough exactly like pastry, working on a lightly-floured board. Raised decoration can be added by brushing the dough lightly with water. Pattern and texture can be worked on the surface of the dough by pressing it with sticks, forks, straw ends, paper-clips, etc. Brush the dough lightly with a wet pastry brush to remove excess flour before baking. Although it is recommended that the salt dough badges be left overnight in an oven set at its lowest setting, the baking process can be speeded up. Baking will take about 2-4 hours (depending on the size of the badge) on a low heat (120°C/350°F/gas mark ½). Do note, salt dough cannot be cooked in a microwave oven.

Papier Mâché

Papier mâché is made from old newspapers and a flour and water paste. The recipe for the flour and water paste varies slightly for the 2 papier mâché projects covered in this book.

Badges For Everyone To make this smooth, slightly runny paste you will need approximately 2 heaped tablespoons of plain white flour to 100 ml water. Gradually add the water to the flour and mix well.

Papier Mâché Pulp Beads To make this smooth, creamy paste you will need approximately 2 heaped tablespoons plain white flour to 200 ml water. Again, gradually add the water to the flour and mix well.

Using a Compass

A compass is a good tool for marking out a perfect circle. The diameter of a circle is the measurement taken across its centre. The compass needs to be fixed at half the measurement of the diameter. If for example a 24-cm diameter circle is needed, use a ruler to measure off 12 cm between the compass point and the compass pencil and fix in position (a screw is normally provided for this). Keep the compass point firmly in contact with the paper and slowly move the pencil arm around to form the circle. Alternatively draw around a dinner plate to make a large circle, or around a jar lid or yoghurt carton for medium-size circles, or around a bottle lid for small circles.

Making a Template

To make a reusable card template, lay a piece of tracing paper over the required template on page 31. Draw around the outline with a pencil. Turn over the tracing paper and scribble over the pencil outline. Turn the tracing paper over once again and lay down onto a piece of thick card. Carefully draw around the pencil outline. Remove the tracing paper. The outline of the traced shape on the card may be quite faint. Go over it with black felt-tip pen. Cut out and label the card template and keep it in a safe place. Use the card template to draw around as many times as is needed onto paper or card.

Swallow is an imprint of Merehurst Limited
Reprinted 1996 by Merehurst Limited
Ferry House, 51-57 Lacy Road, Putney, London SW15 1PR

© Copyright 1993 Merehurst Limited
ISBN 1 898018 10 3

Project Editor: Cheryl Brown
Designer: Anita Ruddell
Photography by Jon Bouchier
Colour separation by Scantrans Pte Limited, Singapore
Printed in Italy by G. Canale & C., S.p.A.

The publisher would like to thank the staff and children of Riversdale Primary School, London Borough of Wandsworth, The Early Learning Centre, Sharjeel Chaudary, Lee Richmond and Jay Darlington for their help in producing the photographs for this book.